DO NOT REMOVE
CARDS FROM POCKET

Super Giants

BILL PARCELLS

by Jerry Carpenter
&
Steve DiMeglio

Edited by Paul J. Deegan

Abdo & Daughters
Minneapolis

1

Published by Abdo & Daughters, 6537 Cecilia Circle, Bloomington, Minnesota 55435

Library bound edition distributed by Rockbottom Books, Pentagon Tower, P.O. Box 36036, Minneapolis, Minnesota 55435

ISBN:0-939179-29-6

Photos — cover: Chris Lauber
pages 3, 6, 9, 12 & 21: Jonathan Daniel
pages 14, 16, 24, 25 & 28: Vernon J. Biever
pages 19 & 32: James Biever

The seconds were ticking away. The Super Bowl was ending. The New York Giants were moments from becoming world champions.

On the sidelines, Giants linebacker Harry Carson was sneaking up behind the head coach. Carson had a huge bucket of Gatorade in his hands. Victory was assured. It was time to celebrate. Carson put the bucket above his head and soaked the head coach with the Gatorade.

Wait a minute. Is this what happens to head coaches in the National Football league (NFL). Are you supposed to shower the coach? In New York you do. Head coach Bill Parcells had a big smile on his face. He was dripping wet. He was a winner. The tradition had continued. When the Giants won in 1986, Parcells got soaked.

"It is fun," Parcells said of the victory baths. "If the players want to have some fun, it is okay with me."

"The shower has become a tradition," Carson once told reporters. "It is always done with affection. Do not think we do not respect him. And do not think he is not the man in charge."

Parcells *is* the man in charge for the Giants. Bill was hired as head coach in 1983. The Giants made the playoffs in 1985, 1986, and 1987. The 1986 season continued until January 1987 when the Giants won the big one — the Super Bowl. They beat the Denver Broncos 39-20 and were NFL champions for the first time since 1963.

The Giants defense was awesome in 1986. Running back Joe Morris was outstanding. Quarterback Phil Simms became a star. Parcells, the coach, was the man that put this all together.

Coach Parcells is different from many of the other coaches in the NFL. He is not flashy. He does not have complex plays. He has fun with his players. No matter what he does, coach Parcells wins.

Corcoran keeps in touch with Parcells today. The Giants head coach sometimes calls his former coach to talk about an upcoming game.

When Parcells was at River Dell, he played quarterback and linebacker on the football team. He was a good baseball catcher. He was a basketball forward who was known to bully his way to the basket.

Parcells stayed with football when he went to college. At Wichita State, Bill was a linebacker. In 1964, the Detroit Lions drafted Parcells in the seventh round.

One of Bill's teammates was drafted by the New York Giants. The Giants were Bill's heroes. He cheered for them as a kid. Parcells wished he could have been drafted by the Giants.

"Four other guys on our team were drafted," Parcells remembered. "One was drafted by the Giants. I was sick. I thought, why could not it have been me?"

Instead of reporting to the Lions, Parcells chose to go to Hastings College in Nebraska as an assistant coach.

At Hastings, he lined the field before practice. After practice, he washed the uniforms. He had to do almost everything.

After Hastings College, Parcells returned to Wichita State as an assistant coach. His long list of coaching jobs was just beginning.

Along the way, Parcells gradually learned what it takes to be a head coach. He learned patience. He learned persistence. He learned to work hard. He learned to get along with players.

From his alma mater, Parcells went to the United States Military Academy at West Point. From Army, he went to Florida State. Then Bill coached at Vanderbilt, then Texas Tech. Finally, Bill landed a head coaching job at the Air Force Academy in Colorado Springs, Colorado. His team went 3-8.

After that single season, Parcells went to the professional ranks, and once again he was an assistant coach. In 1980 he was the linebackers coach for the New England Patriots of the American Football Conference.

A year later, Parcells finally got to the Giants. He was hired as the team's defensive coordinator. The Giants qualified for the playoffs after that 1981 season.

It was a dream come true for Parcells to go to New York. As a kid, the Giants were his heroes. They played in the city at the time. Bill sat in the lower right field stands at Yankee Stadium and watched the Giants. He had watched his first Giants football game from the Polo Grounds bleachers in 1954.

He went to about 15 games when he was growing up. When he could not go to a game, he would listen on the radio. In 1958, the Giants played for the championship. Bill sat in the car on a wintery day and listened to the game. The Giants lost to the Colts. Bill was heartbroken.

Bill kept cheering for the Giants. He kept wishing some day he would coach them. His dream would come true.

Parcells was named the Giants head coach after Ray Perkins resigned. Parcells had moved to the top of the coaching ranks. "I always had it in my heart that I wanted to coach the Giants," Parcells said. "It is a corny thing, but it is true."

"Not too many people get to do what they want to do and have it turn out exactly the way they dreamed," Parcells noted.

"It meant something for him to coach the Giants. That was a plus," Giants general manager George Young recalled about the hiring. However, that first season was a nightmare for Bill and the Giants.

The Giants had a 3-12-1 record in 1983. There were many injuries. New York struggled.

Tragedies also plagued the Giants. Running back Doug Kotar died of a brain tumor.

Offensive backfield coach Bob Ledbetter died of a stroke. Personally, both of Parcells' parents died in 1983.

The first season was difficult, but Parcells was determined to move forward. He wanted to succeed as a head coach in the NFL.

The Giants management stood by Parcells and he got the job done. The Giants were 9-7 in 1984 and made the playoffs. They won the first playoff game, but lost in the second round.

In 1985 the Giants were 10-6 and again in the playoffs. The Giants beat the San Francisco 49ers 17-3 in the first playoff game. Chicago ended the Giants year in the second playoff game as the Bears beat the Giants 21-0. The Bears went on to win the Super Bowl.

In 1986 it was the Giants who went to the Super Bowl. They won it all. New York went 14-2 in the regular season. In the playoffs, the Giants first crushed the 49ers 49-3. New York won the National Football Conference title

game with a 17-0 decision over the Washington Redskins.

In the Super Bowl, the Giants beat Denver 39-20 to become the world champions.

Driving the players to the championship was Parcells. Many of Bill's ideas helped turn the franchise around. The Giants went from losers to winners. It had been a long time between championships for New York.

Parcell's philosophy about defense brought back the glory days. In the 1950's, the familiar chants of "DEE-fense, DEE-fense, DEE-fense" were heard in the rafters of Yankee Stadium. Many pro football observers think Giants fans invented that chant in the mid-1950s.

The Giants were one of the first NFL teams to glamorize defense. The 1950s were the days of Sam Huff, Andy Robustelli, Roosevelt Grier, Jim Katcavage, and Emlen Tunnell. These men and others made defensive players larger-than-life heroes.

Parcells brought back the glamour.

"Our feeling on defense is that you have to stop the run first," Parcells has said about defense.

Giants assistant coach Bill Belichick has the same thoughts: "We have a pretty big team physically. We look for size first. We want to force the other team to throw."

That is the Giants — big and strong. Tough players dictate the way the game is played. The Giants are physical. The Giants are a strong team. They spend many hours in the weight room. Parcells was instrumental in getting management to build a new weight room. He thinks the added emphasis on weight training has been a key to the Giants success.

Jim Burt, Lawrence Taylor, Leonard Marshall, Harry Carson, George Martin. These and other Giants have become larger-than-life heroes. They are a very good defensive unit. They draw praise from opposing coaches.

19

"It is not hard to prepare a game plan for the Giants because they use such a basic alignment," Dallas head coach Tom Landry has said. But, Landy added, even though "you know where they are, they are just very hard to control."

Ted Plumb is an assistant coach with the Philadelphia Eagles. He says of the Giants defense: "They keep coming after you, and the more the game goes on, the less effective the offense is."

Parcells has also improved the offense. In New York, the media pressure is tremendous. The media kept saying quarterback Phil Simms had to be replaced. However, Bill had faith in Simms. Phil was going to be Parcells quarterback. The decision turned out to be a wise one.

Simms led the Giants to the Super Bowl championship. He has been an All-Pro two years in a row. He has become a top NFL quarterback.

Another offensive player that Parcells helped was running back Joe Morris. In Bill's first

year as head coach in 1983, he decided to give one running back the full time job. The Giants running attack had been terrible. Bill picked Morris to change that.

One day Bill said to Joe: "We need you. We have to open up our offense. We need your speed and quickness and cutting ability and breakaway skills. You are in there full-time."

In Joe's first start, he scored three touchdowns. Parcell's move paid off. Joe became a star. Morris broke the Giants rushing record in 1985. A season later, he broke his own rushing record.

Lawrence Taylor entered a drug treatment center in March of 1986. Parcells helped him through the problem. He helped arrange Taylor's treatment. He stood by Taylor. He also respected Taylor's privacy on the subject.

"Bill helped me more than anyone else," Taylor has said. "I have to thank him for giving me strength." Taylor came to camp in the fall of 1986 ready to concentrate on football. He made a major contribution in the Giants championship season.

Taylor is a star, but Parcells stands by all his players. He tries to talk to every player every day. He jokes with some of them. He pats them on the back.

"I love kidding around with them," Parcells once said about his players. "It makes me feel 25 years old." Parcells was 45 years old as the 1987 season began.

Giants players like him as a coach. They also respect Parcells. They play hard for him. He is known to them as "Bill." They admire his philosophy that his job is to give them the best possible chance to win.

"What really makes him stand out is that he is such a great manager of people. Handling people is more important than designing plays for a head coach," wide receiver Phil McConkey has said about Parcells.

"He is more or less one of us," Harry Carson said about Parcells. "He is a players-type coach."

"He is pretty easygoing," Lawrence Taylor said about the coach. "He takes a lot of pride in his team. He demands you work hard."

Parcells can also make players dislike him. He sometimes does this on purpose to fire them up. He does it to motivate the players. He wants them to play better. He does this by yelling at certain players. He singles them out. He embarrasses them. Then they want to prove they can play well.

"Bill is a great motivator," Carson said. "He knows exactly what to say. He knows what things will really get to you."

Parcells did this with Jim Burt. Burt is the starting nose tackle for the Giants. Parcells once told Burt he was not doing his job. Burt got mad. He took it out on the opponents in the next game. Then he got revenge on Parcells. He was the first player to dump water on the coach.

Not only does he get dunked regularly, Parcells also is superstitious.

Parcells learned all about superstitions from his mother. One of them concerns elephants. In Bill's office at Giants Stadium, he has 10 toy or brass elephants on shelves. The elephants' trunks are up. They face the door. This is supposed to bring good luck.

Also, Bill has one penny in his locker. He has another penny just outside his locker. Parcells refuses to touch them. He thinks it would bring bad luck.

Every day on his way to work, Parcells picks up two cups of coffee at a diner. He then buys two more cups of coffee at another diner. He does this every day on his way to the stadium. Parcells says this is just habit. Many people feel it is just another superstition for Parcells.

One day as he was driving to work, a black cat crossed his path. This, of course, is suppose to bring bad luck. Bill's mother taught him how to erase this trouble. So Bill backed up his car over the spot where the cat had walked.

"That means I erased it," Parcells said. "That means it never crossed my path."

Bill Parcells is not an ordinary coach. He is a friend to his players. He eats at diners. He is not fancy. He is not flashy. He is superstitious. But above all, he wins.

In 1986 Parcells also erased memories of his first year as the Giants head coach. He proved he was a winner. In key games along the way he made gutsy calls that helped the Giants win. A big one came in a Monday night game at San Francisco.

The Giants were behind 17-0 at halftime. The 49ers had stopped Morris and the Giants offense. Parcells made changes in the second half. He switched the game plan away from Morris and put it in Simms' hands. The Giants offense opened up. Simms passed the Giants to a 21-17 victory.

A big play in the game came when Parcells called for a fourth down run. The Giants were behind 17-7 and had fourth down and two yards to go. Instead of punting, Parcells told the offense to run the ball. If the play failed, the Giants probably would have lost.

Parcells kept the punting team on the sidelines. He later said he had a "gut feeling." Simms handed the ball to Morris. Joe gained 17 yards. The Giants were on their way. The gamble paid off.

In the January 1987 Super Bowl, Parcells ordered another running play on fourth down. The Giants were trailing 10-9 early in the second half. It was fourth down. One yard to go.

Parcells sent in his punting unit this time. But at the last second, reserve quarterback Jeff Rutledge moved up under the center. He took the snap and sneaked for the first down. Five plays later, Simms hit tight end Mark Bavaro for the go-ahead touchdown. The assault was on. The Giants rolled to the 39-20 victory.

"You are trying to win the game," the coach said about the Super Bowl call. "That was for the world championship. So you take your shot."

Parcells downplays his success. Parcells said the players deserve the credit. He does not want the attention. However, he was named the NFL Coach Of the Year for 1986.

"Let me tell you something," Parcells has said. "All those guys that are great coaches, it is because they have got really good players. That is what it is. You get good players, you organize them, then all of a sudden you win."

After the championship season ended, Parcells said, "I am not interested in being known around the country. I will just hang around Hackensack, New Jersey."

It is too late. The country knows Bill Parcells now. They know he is easy going. That he is not flashy. That he is down-home, a blue collar guy who has truck drivers for friends.

Most of all, football fans throughout the country know that Parcells is a good coach. Fans know Parcells turned the Giants around, and that he coached them to the world championship in Super Bowl XXI.